THE THREE WISHES

Retold by Lynne Benton

Illustrated by Kevin McAleenan

Heinemann

Once upon a time a woodcutter and his wife lived in a forest. They worked as hard as they could but they were very poor.

One day, as the woodcutter was working, an old woman came up to him. She wanted to buy a lot of wood.

The woodcutter put the wood in a big sack.

'This is very heavy,' he said to her.

'Let me carry the sack for you.'

'You are very kind,' said the old woman.

So the woodcutter carried the sack of wood to the old woman's cottage.

When they got to her cottage the old woman said, ‘Thank you for carrying my wood. Now I will do something for you. I will give you and your wife three wishes. But don’t forget to think before you wish.’

The woodcutter thanked the old woman. Then he smiled and said to himself, 'She is just an old woman. How can she give us three wishes?'

Then he went back to work and forgot all about her.

By the end of the day the woodcutter was tired and very hungry.

'I hope my wife has made something nice for tea,' he said to himself.

But when he got home the only thing to eat was some bread.
The woodcutter was cross.
'I have worked hard all day and I'm very hungry,' he said.
His wife said, 'We are too poor to buy anything nice for tea.'

‘I know we are poor,’ said the woodcutter. ‘But I am very hungry. I wish I had a sausage to eat.’ Suddenly a big fat sausage lay on the table. It looked very good.

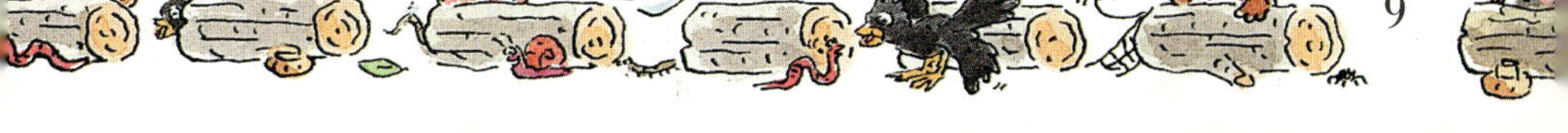

‘Where did that sausage come from?’
asked the woodcutter’s wife.
‘I think I know,’ said the woodcutter.
‘An old woman gave me three wishes
and I forgot all about them!’

'You silly man!' shouted his wife. 'You could have wished for lots of food to eat ...

... or a nice house to live in ...

... or lots of money.

But you wished for a sausage!'

‘Now our first wish has gone,’ said his wife. ‘Oooh! I am so cross. I wish that sausage was on the end of your nose!’

Suddenly the big fat sausage jumped off the table and on to the end of the woodcutter’s nose.

‘Now look!’ said the woodcutter. ‘Because of you we have lost another wish. Help me to pull the sausage off my nose.’

So they pulled and pulled but the sausage would not come off.

'You silly woman,' said the woodcutter. 'We must wish the sausage off or it will be there for ever.'

So the woodcutter said, 'I wish the sausage would come off my nose now!'

Suddenly the big fat sausage fell off his nose and back on to the table.

'That was our last wish,' said the woodcutter sadly.

'I'm sorry I got cross,' he said to his wife.

'And I'm sorry I shouted,' said his wife.

'We have been very silly,' they said.

'We still have the sausage to eat,' said the woodcutter.

So they cut the sausage in two and ate it with the bread.

'That was the best sausage I have ever had,' said the woodcutter. 'But if we ever have three wishes again, we will think before we wish.'